VOYAGER
—— TO THE ——
PLANETS

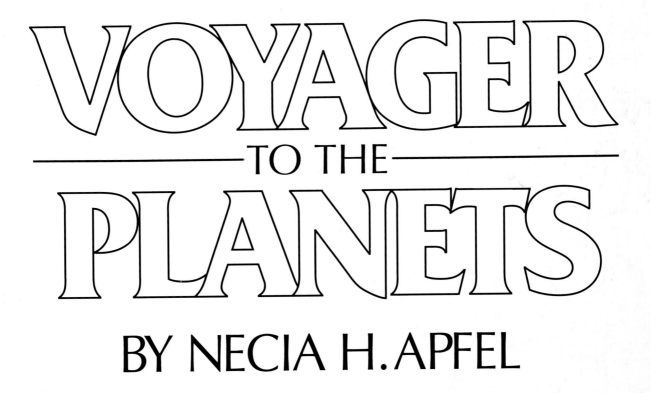

VOYAGER
TO THE
PLANETS

BY NECIA H. APFEL

CLARION BOOKS • NEW YORK

The photograph on page 46 was taken by the author.
All others are courtesy of JPL-NASA.

Clarion Books
a Houghton Mifflin Company imprint
215 Park Avenue South, New York, NY 10003
Copyright © 1991 by Necia H. Apfel

Library of Congress Cataloging-in-Publication Data
Apfel, Necia H.
Voyager to the planets / Necia H. Apfel.
p.   cm.
Includes bibliographical references and index.
Summary: Examines the development and travels of the space
probes Voyager I and Voyager II and the information they have
provided since the first launch in 1977.
ISBN 0-395-55209-5   PA ISBN 0-395-69622-4
1. Project Voyager—Juvenile literature.
2. Planets—Exploration—Juvenile literature.
[1. Project Voyager.   2. Outer space—Exploration]   I. Title.
TL789.8.U6V52462   1990
523.4—dc20   90-45057
CIP AC
BVG 10 9 8 7 6 5 4 3 2

*Title page photograph: The planet Saturn with its moons Tethys and Dione,
photographed from 21 million kilometers (13 million miles) away.
Note the shadows cast on Saturn by its rings.
Photograph on facing page: After flying past Neptune, Voyager took one
of its last pictures of this planet.*

To Steve, Mimi, and Andy—
and, of course, my grandson Ben

ar beyond the farthest planets in our solar system two small spacecraft are sailing through outer space. Their names are Voyager 1 and Voyager 2. They were designed and built over a period of more than ten years by teams of scientists and engineers. The Voyagers had to be strong enough for their very long and difficult journeys. The spacecraft had to be able to withstand the frigid and airless conditions of space. They had to carry many different instruments to gather information about planets they would visit. They also needed instruments to send the data back to the scientists on Earth. All of these instruments had to be sturdy enough to keep operating in space for at least four years and possibly even longer.

The Voyagers were not the first spacecraft to be sent to collect data about planets in our solar system. In 1962 Mariner 2, launched from the United States, flew by the planet Venus. Since then all the planets except Pluto have been visited by spacecraft at least once. But no spacecraft before Voyager 2 flew by more than two planets.

The idea of a Grand Tour of all the outer planets developed in the 1960s. Astronomers found that if they carefully aimed a spacecraft toward a particular point near a planet, they could use the planet's gravitational effect on the spacecraft to redirect its path. Such gravity-assists can enable a spacecraft to planet-hop—visit perhaps three or four planets, one after the other. But this is possible only when the selected planets are in the right positions in their orbits. That special alignment only happens about once every 175 years.

The planet Jupiter and its four largest moons: Io (top left), Europa (center), Ganymede (lower left), and Callisto (lower right)

Originally four craft were to be built for the Grand Tour project, but budget pressures required the National Aeronautics and Space Administration (NASA) to limit the scope of the mission. Now two spacecraft were to be built and both sent to Jupiter and Saturn. A third craft that was later to go to Jupiter and Uranus was never built.

At first the mission was called the Mariner-Jupiter-Saturn project, or MJS77 for short. It was approved by Congress in 1972 and was renamed the Voyager Project in 1977 before the spacecraft were launched.

Although they were disappointed by the cutbacks in the program, the mission designers for MJS77 knew it might be possible to revive the Grand Tour dream later. The Voyagers could be sent on to Uranus and Neptune after they had reached Saturn. But instead of sending Voyager 1 on the Grand Tour, astronomers decided to let it take a better look at Titan, Saturn's largest moon. The spacecraft's close flyby past Titan put it on a path that did not allow the gravity-assist required to direct it toward Uranus.

Even so, Voyager 1's journey was deemed an enormous success. As Voyager 2 neared Saturn in its turn, NASA officials agreed it should complete the Grand Tour by going on to Uranus and Neptune. Unfortunately, it was not possible to arrange a gravity-assist at Neptune to send Voyager to Pluto.

Let us follow the adventures of this remarkable spacecraft from the time it left Earth. On August 20, 1977, Voyager 2 was placed atop a Titan 3-E/Centaur rocket at the United States launching site on Cape Canaveral in Florida. The rocket blasted off and rose majestically into the clear blue sky.

All was well. But now the real countdown began. Voyager 2 would take two years to reach its first destination—the giant planet Jupiter.

Voyager 2 liftoff,
August 20, 1977

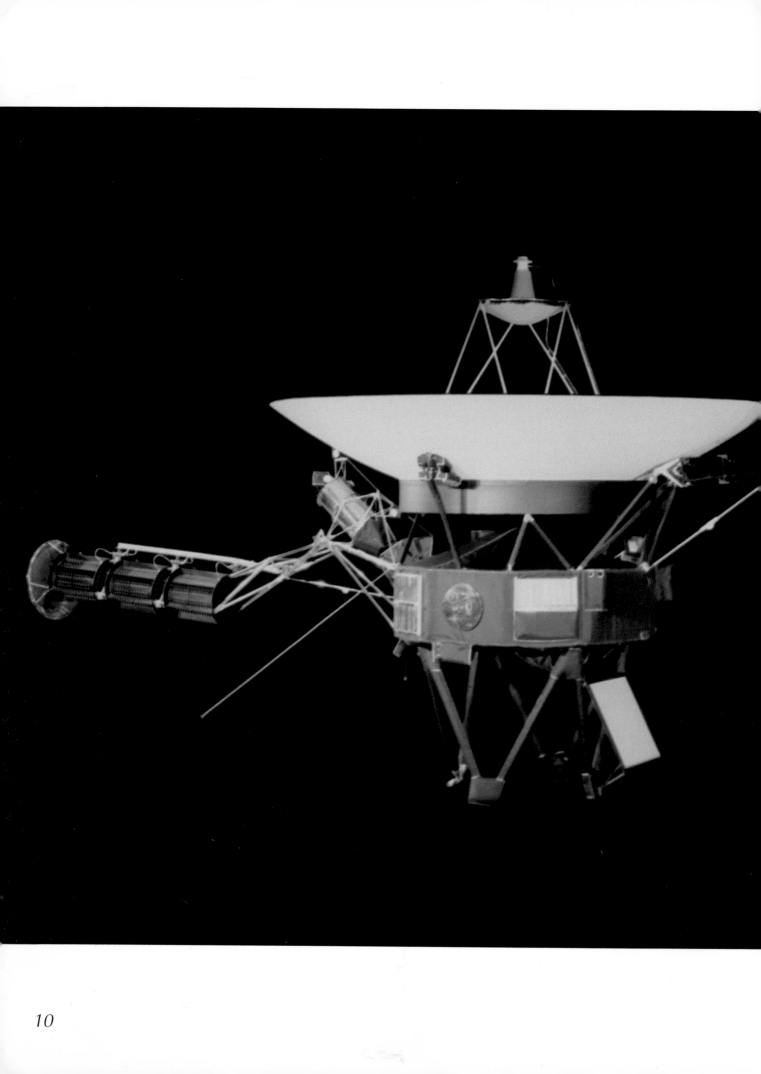

The Voyager spacecraft

Voyager is a strange-looking machine with tubes and boxlike structures sticking out all over it. These contain its many instruments, including cameras, radio receivers, and ultraviolet and infrared sensors. The instruments were designed to collect data from places Voyager would visit and to send this information back to Earth, where scientists and engineers were eagerly awaiting the reports.

Sometimes instructions had to be sent from stations on Earth to Voyager, telling it when to change its position, what data to record, or which instruments to use. Voyager was equipped with a big umbrella-shaped antenna to receive these directions.

In designing Voyager, the engineers tried very hard to anticipate any problems or emergencies that might arise on its long journey. But the first difficulty occurred much sooner than they expected. Only eight months after Voyager was launched, its primary radio system stopped working and the backup radio receiver developed a short circuit. These defects drastically reduced Voyager's ability to receive instructions from the scientists. New computer programs had to be sent to Voyager so that it could respond to future commands. The scientists could only hope that the defective radio system would last for the entire journey. Otherwise, there would be no way for them to communicate with Voyager.

With its faulty radio operating weakly, Voyager kept sailing farther into space. After two years it finally arrived at the colorfully banded planet Jupiter, passing closest to it on July 9, 1979.

Jupiter is so big that more than 1,300 Earths could fit inside of it. It has more material in it than all the other planets in the solar system combined. It is truly a giant planet.

Following commands from programmers on Earth, Voyager took pictures of Jupiter's clouds, recorded their temperatures and speeds, and analyzed their composition. The spacecraft found that it is very cold out there, a half-billion miles from the sun. Jupiter receives only one twenty-fifth the sunlight we receive on Earth. Its pretty clouds have temperatures of about –145° C (–230° F). Deep inside Jupiter it is much warmer, and at the planet's center the temperature rises to 30,000° C (54,000° F). That's around five times as hot as the surface of the sun, where it is about 6,000° C (11,000° F).

This great heat rising from the interior would make Jupiter's cloud tops look like a multicolored bubbling mixture if the planet were not turning around rapidly on its axis. But Jupiter rotates very fast. A day on Jupiter lasts only ten hours. This rapid rotation causes the clouds to be pulled out into a series of colored bands. Different substances in the clouds give them their varied colors.

(Right) The giant planet Jupiter, photographed from 37 million kilometers (23 million miles) away. The Great Red Spot appears at the extreme left edge of the planet. (Below) Close-up of Jupiter's cloud movements

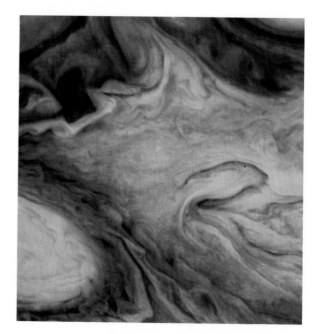

The bands of clouds circling Jupiter are not smooth or featureless. Within them are huge, turbulent storms, whirlpools, and other disturbances. Weather on this giant planet is extremely violent and forceful. The most noticeable storm is called the Great Red Spot. It is so big that it can be observed through telescopes on Earth and has been seen for at least three hundred years.

Long before Voyager was launched, astronomers knew that the Great Red Spot was a giant storm, towering 16 kilometers (10 miles) above the rest of the clouds that swirl around it. Through their telescopes, they had seen the Red Spot change in size and in brightness, although it never seemed to vanish completely. Voyager's pictures showed the Red Spot to be about the size of Earth, but at other times it was known to be three times the size of Earth. Its color also varied from bright cherry red to very faint reddish hues. Astronomers aren't sure why the Great Red Spot appears red or why it has lasted such a long time.

Although the Great Red Spot drifts around the planet, it is always about the same distance below Jupiter's equator. As it drifts, it also rotates, taking about six days to turn around once. This rotation and drifting cause the gases around the Red Spot to eddy and swirl, somewhat like the way rocks and other barriers cause a rapidly rushing stream of water to froth and foam into small whirlpools and eddies. The photographs taken by Voyager show these eddies and swirls in great detail.

Jupiter is the center of its own miniature solar system. It has at least sixteen moons, three of which were discovered by Voyager. Four of Jupiter's moons are very large, with diameters of several thousands of miles. The other twelve moons are no bigger than a few hundred miles across, and many are much smaller.

Although Voyager took photographs of Jupiter's smaller moons, most of its attention was concentrated on the planet's four large moons. These were first discovered by the Italian astronomer Galileo in 1610, and so are called the Galilean moons. They can be seen with a small telescope as small white points of light. But the close-up photographs taken by Voyager showed us what these moons really look like.

A close-up of Jupiter's Great Red Spot surrounded by other turbulent cloud formations

One of Voyager's major discoveries was that the innermost Galilean moon, Io, has the highest level of volcanism in the entire solar system. Nine active volcanoes are almost continuously spouting hot liquid sulfur more than 100 kilometers (62 miles) into space at very high speeds. No volcano on Earth ejects lava at such tremendous velocity.

The ejected sulfur cools quickly in the frigid void of space and falls back down, coating Io's surface with hues of white, yellow, orange, and red. Some observers have dubbed Io the pizza pie moon, because of the many warm colors and strange shapes on its surface.

Because Io's surface is constantly being covered with sulfur, it keeps changing. It has no old craters or other ancient markings like those found on our moon and on many other satellites Voyager visited later in its journey.

The second Galilean moon from Jupiter is called Europa. Astronomers knew it was the smallest of these four large

(Above) A massive volcanic eruption on Io's horizon that sent debris 160 kilometers (100 miles) high. (Below) A mosaic (composite) photograph of Jupiter's moon Io

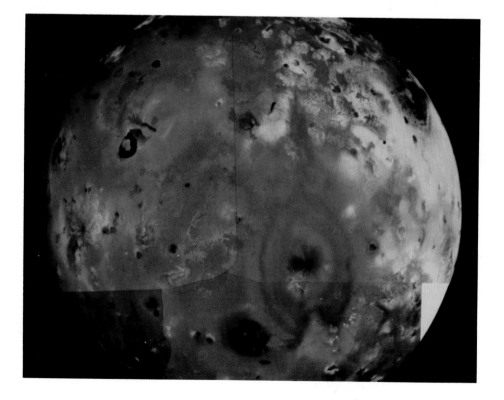

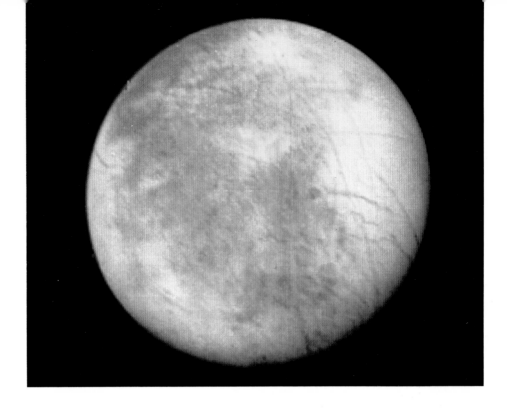

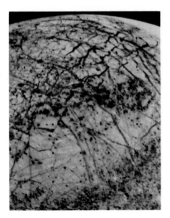

(Above) Jupiter's moon Europa from two million kilometers (1.2 million miles) away. (Below) Note its lined surface, which showed up very clearly when Voyager was only 240,000 kilometers (150,000 miles) away.

satellites. Voyager's photographs revealed that Europa is also the smoothest object in the solar system. It has no mountains or even cliffs. In fact, there is nothing on it higher than about 150 feet. It is so smooth it has been called the billiard ball moon, although in proportion to its size, it is actually smoother than a billiard ball.

Europa has dark lines or stripes crisscrossing its surface, but these stand out from the surface no more than felt-tip pen marks on a billiard ball. They are just cracks in Europa's thick icy crust. Darker material from below seeped up through these cracks, filled them in, and froze, creating the dark lines.

The ice covering Europa's entire surface may extend down many miles. Underneath this thick frigid layer may be a deep ocean. Astronomers are not sure of the depth of Europa's frozen crust and ocean, but they do know that there is a hard rocky core beneath the ice and water. It is likely that Europa has no mountains or cliffs because its surface is primarily made of ice, which cannot support as much weight as rocks or metallic substances and tends to flatten out over time. That is what scientists believe happened on Europa.

The third and largest of the Galilean moons is called Ganymede. It is nearly as big as the red planet Mars. Voyager found that Ganymede is completely different from both Io and Europa. For example, it has some dark areas containing many small craters as well as several very large ones. One of these large craters is about 3,250 kilometers (2,000 miles) in diameter. One of Voyager's photographs showed the crater clearly with many closely spaced bands crisscrossing its surface.

Other lighter-colored regions on Ganymede look from afar like parallel grooves. Actually they are straight ridges of low mountains and valleys. The mountains are low because Ganymede, like Europa, has a lot of ice in its makeup. In fact, one-half of the material in this large moon is ice. But on Ganymede the ice is mixed with rocky matter, which gives the small mountains enough support to maintain their structure.

(Above) Jupiter's moon Ganymede from 1.2 million kilometers (744,000 miles) away. Note the enormous crater spanning more than one-half the moon's width. (Below) A closer look at Ganymede, this time from 243,000 kilometers (152,000 miles) away

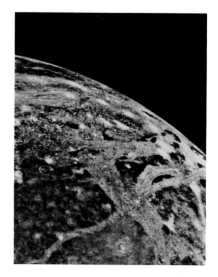

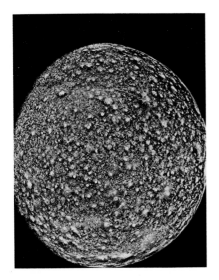

Jupiter's moon Callisto from 392,000 kilometers (245,000 miles) away. Compare its rugged, cratered surface with that of Europa. (Below) Callisto from 2.3 million kilometers (1.4 million miles) away. The white splotches may be ice thrown out by ancient impacts upon the very dark surface.

Like Ganymede, the fourth and outermost Galilean moon, Callisto, is a mixture of half ice and half rock. But very little ice was actually seen in Voyager's photographs of Callisto. Instead, Voyager found its entire surface very dark and very cratered.

These craters were formed billions of years ago. At that time, large chunks of rock crashed into all the planets and moons, creating holes of every size. On some bodies, such as Earth, rain and wind eroded most evidence of these ancient impacts. Io's volcanoes effectively covered any traces of craters long ago. But on Callisto no such changes have taken place. This moon has so many craters that no new one can be formed without destroying an old one. Because Callisto is so cratered, we know that its surface is very old, billions of years old.

Callisto's craters are not very deep, however, because the ice that makes up one-half of its composition can't support tall walls or high cliffs. Earth's moon, which is about the same size as Callisto, has much deeper holes and higher walls. But our moon has no ice to weaken its structure.

Jupiter's rings and a thin curve of the planet's horizon are illuminated by sunlight com.

We now know that all four of the planets visited by Voyager have ring systems. Saturn's magnificent ring system was discovered about 1610 by Galileo, the discoverer of Jupiter's four large moons. In 1977, more than 350 years later, faint rings around the planet Uranus were detected through powerful telescopes. Astronomers started theorizing that perhaps Jupiter and Neptune also had ring systems. Voyager proved them right when it discovered rings around both planets.

From afar, all these ring systems appear solid, but they are actually composed of thousands of individual chunks of ice, all following similar orbits around a planet. Saturn's rings are the most spectacular, but all four ring systems are fascinating in different ways.

Voyager found that Jupiter's ring system is just a single ring consisting of several parts with no gaps between them. The brightest part is the outer edge, but even this section is too faint to be detected from Earth. Just outside this edge Voyager found two very small moons. Both moons race rapidly around Jupiter, taking only about seven hours to complete their orbits. By contrast, our moon takes twenty-nine and one-half days to orbit Earth, which is a much smaller planet.

By moving so quickly, these tiny moons prevent any ring particles from straying beyond the ring's outer edge, farther out into space. Astronomers call such moons shepherd satellites because, like sheep dogs with sheep, they keep ring particles confined within certain regions.

Because no shepherd satellites control the inner particles of Jupiter's ring system, they have spread out very thinly, reaching all the way to Jupiter's cloud tops. Only when Voyager was very close to Jupiter could it detect this faint, wispy diffusion of tiny particles.

om behind the planet.

Leaving Jupiter, Voyager headed farther into the frigid emptiness of space. For two more years it traveled outward another half-billion miles, reaching the ringed planet Saturn in August 1981.

Saturn's rapid rotation, like Jupiter's, causes its clouds to appear as colorful bands. But Saturn has no giant storms like Jupiter's Great Red Spot. It has much smaller storms that look brown and white in Voyager's photographs.

Saturn also has much less material in it than Jupiter. In fact, although it is the second largest planet and has a diameter ten times that of Earth, it is a lightweight planet. Saturn is so light that it would actually float on water if it were put into a swimming pool large enough to hold it.

A thick layer of haze covers Saturn, making its atmospheric markings look much more muted than Jupiter's. Its clouds appear in different shades of butterscotch rather than bright orange, yellow, and white.

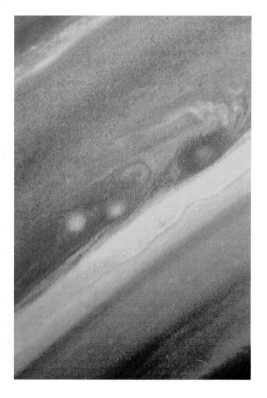

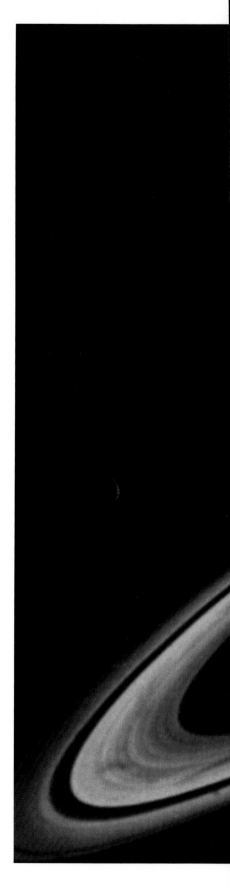

(Left) A small section of Saturn's northern hemisphere from 7 million kilometers (4.4 million miles) away. Note the small storms within the bands of clouds. Color has been enhanced to bring out more detail. (Right) Saturn from 21 million kilometers (13 million miles) away. Saturn's moons Tethys, Dione, and Rhea can be seen below the planet.

Nothing obscures Saturn's magnificent rings. Billions of icy particles orbit the planet in a flat sheet, extending outward more than 75,000 kilometers (45,000 miles). But the thickness of this sheet is only about one hundred yards, the length of a football field. The rings cast shadows on Saturn's clouds but are thin enough for stars to be seen through them, even from Earth.

From Earth the rings appear to be divided into a few discrete sections. Voyager found that each section contained many thousands of narrow "ringlets." Most of these ringlets are only 1 to 10 kilometers (1/2 mile to 6 miles) wide. Although there are no completely empty gaps between the ringlets, some areas are nearly empty, creating natural separations or edges. As Voyager had found at Jupiter, shepherd satellites help herd the tiny particles of Saturn's rings into confined orbits.

The particles in the rings range from dust-size grains to blocks of ice as big as houses. Most, however, are about half an inch across. Color and size appear to vary with the location of the particles, although the reason for this differentiation is not yet known.

Although the rings are most impressive looking, they are not very substantial. If somehow all the ice particles were melted and then refrozen into a solid sheet the same size as the original ring system, that sheet would only be about 50 centimeters (20 inches) thick.

(Left) The many rings of Saturn. Color variations indicate different chemical compositions. (Below) A small section of Saturn's rings. Larger particles can be detected among the many ringlets.

Saturn, like Jupiter, has its own solar system, with at least eighteen moons. But Saturn has only one large moon, Titan. The rest are quite small. Eight of these have been called "moonlets" or "the Rocks" because they are very tiny, irregular chunks of rocky material. Some of them are shepherd satellites.

Titan, on the other hand, is bigger than the planet Mercury. It is also the only moon in the solar system that has a thick atmosphere. This atmosphere is so thick, in fact, that Voyager couldn't see Titan's surface at all. Titan's atmosphere is mainly nitrogen, much like Earth's atmosphere, which also contains oxygen. Titan lacks oxygen, the element so vital to life on Earth.

Beneath its thick, smoglike clouds, Titan's surface must be a dark, gloomy place, much like the depths of an ocean on Earth. Because of its nitrogen atmosphere, Titan may be the way Earth was billions of years ago, before life appeared. Of course, Titan is much colder than Earth ever was. Its surface temperature is around −182°C (−296° F). Titan is also much smaller than Earth. Its diameter is only about 6,000 kilometers (3,700 miles). Earth is more than twice as big.

(Left) Saturn's largest moon, Titan, from 435,000 kilometers (270,000) miles) away. Very little detail can be seen through the thick haze that covers the entire moon. (Right) Titan. The only noticeable detail is the lighter color in the moon's northern hemisphere.

The seven biggest moons of Saturn had been discovered through telescopes on Earth long before Voyager took off on its journey. Voyager found the other eleven moons and was able to take many close-up photographs, which revealed details too small to be seen from Earth. Like Jupiter's moons, each of Saturn's was found to have its own peculiarities.

For example, Saturn's small moon Mimas is very heavily cratered. One crater covers one-third of its surface. An enormous object must have crashed into Mimas to make this crater; anything larger would have completely destroyed this moon.

Tethys, Saturn's second largest moon, has a crater that is actually larger than Mimas.

Saturn's moon Mimas from 129,000 kilometers (80,000 miles) away. Its enormous crater is not visible in this picture but can be seen in the jacket photograph.

Saturn's moon Tethys. Note the long canyon extending from top to bottom near the right-hand edge of the moon.

Enceladus, the brightest moon in the solar system, as seen from 74,000 kilometers (46,000 miles) away

Saturn's battered moon Hyperion

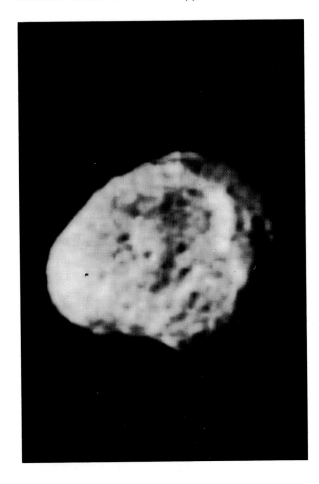

Tethys also has a 2,000-kilometer (1,200-mile)-long canyon extending three-fourths of the way around it. Then there is the moon Enceladus, not much bigger than Mimas, but with very few craters and covered with extremely pure white ice. This covering gives it the brightest surface of all the moons in the solar system.

Hyperion, another small moon, is only 360 kilometers (223 miles) at its widest dimension. It is battered and misshapen due to many collisions with other objects. Because it is so small, its gravity isn't strong enough to pull it into a more spherical shape, which might happen with a larger body. Some say Hyperion looks like a well-done hamburger or a bashed hockey puck.

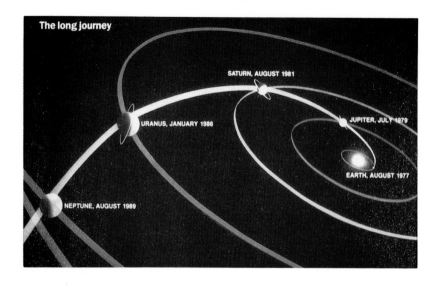

The long journey

SATURN, AUGUST 1981

URANUS, JANUARY 1986

JUPITER, JULY 1979

EARTH, AUGUST 1977

NEPTUNE, AUGUST 1989

Diagram of Voyager 2's twelve-year journey as it visited Jupiter, Saturn, Uranus, and Neptune

The Voyager mission was planned only as four-year flights to Jupiter and Saturn. Voyager 1 had already gathered a great amount of information about those two planets and was now headed out of the solar system. Voyager 2 was still in reasonable operating condition, and therefore the engineers reprogrammed its flight path as it approached Saturn. They decided to send it on to the planets Uranus and Neptune. Voyager was carefully aimed so that Saturn could give it a gravity-assist change of direction toward Uranus.

Before Voyager 2 reached Uranus, however, the engineers found that the spacecraft had lost much of the lubricant needed to keep its scanning platform operating. Without the ability to turn easily, the cameras mounted on this platform could not be aimed properly. Instead, the entire spacecraft would have to be rotated, a much more difficult maneuver. Also, Voyager's computer software, especially those commands controlling Voyager's stabilization and photographing instructions, had to be redesigned.

The engineers knew that whereas Voyager had been able to spend several days at Jupiter and Saturn, it would have only about six hours at Uranus. And because Uranus is so much farther from the sun than either Jupiter or Saturn, much, much less sunlight reaches it. Taking a picture at Uranus has been compared to photographing a ball park at night by the light of a single candle.

The engineers calculated that Voyager would be moving at about 12 miles per second (43,000 miles per hour) when it went past Uranus. This meant that in 10 seconds it would move 120 miles. So Voyager's camera had to be moved backward at just the right speed to compensate for this rapid forward motion. All these commands had to be sent to Voyager almost three hours beforehand, because that's how long it takes light or radio waves, traveling at the speed of light (300,000 kilometers or 186,000 miles per second), to reach the planet from Earth.

Also, because of the increased distance, Voyager's radio signals back to Earth became much weaker. The engineers had to expand the Deep Space Network that tracked and communicated with Voyager. To do this, they started using powerful radio telescopes, such as the Very Large Array (VLA) in New Mexico and a similar one in Australia. These large series of connected radio telescopes act as one huge telescope, detecting radio waves too faint for a single receiver to pick up. Once again, when Voyager had in effect radioed home for help, the engineers were able to devise new and brilliant solutions. Voyager's engineers were the real heroes of this story.

The Very Large Array (VLA) in New Mexico. Each of the twenty-seven radio telescopes is 26 meters (85 feet) across and is mounted on railroad tracks 21 kilometers (13 miles) long.

All these preparations took place while Voyager silently traveled onward. On January 24, 1986, after four and a half long years, the sturdy spacecraft came within about 80,000 kilometers (50,000 miles) of Uranus. It was only 16 kilometers (10 miles) off the desired point after having traveled 3¼ billion kilometers (2 billion miles) from Earth.

Uranus was discovered during the time of the American Revolutionary War. In 1781, the English astronomer Sir William Herschel realized that what previously had been recorded as a star was actually the seventh planet in our solar system. Many years later, five moons were found orbiting Uranus, and then in 1977 Uranus's ring system was detected.

Uranus's main peculiarity, however, was known long before Voyager's journey. It is not the planet's rings or its moons that are unique. It is the planet itself. Unlike other planets, which rotate in an upright position, Uranus rolls along in its orbit like a top spinning on its side. As a result, during half of its eighty-four-year orbit Uranus's north pole faces the sun, and during the other half its south pole is sunlit. Uranus's moons and rings also follow this strange orientation because they all have orbits directly above Uranus's equator.

Astronomers were disappointed at how few features Voyager was able to detect in Uranus's clouds. Layers of thick haze hang over most of the upper clouds, obscuring any details that may exist below. A small amount of methane gas in the haze and clouds gives the planet its soft blue-green color.

(Above) Uranus from 9 million kilometers (5.7 million miles) away. Very few features are visible on this haze-covered planet.
(Right) A simulated view over the horizon of Uranus's moon Miranda showing the planet and its rings

(Left) Uranus's ten rings from 1.1 million kilometers (690,000 miles). The outermost ring, at top of photograph, is actually two distinct rings lying very close together. (Right) Two shepherd satellites keep Uranus's outermost ring particles in their narrow orbits.

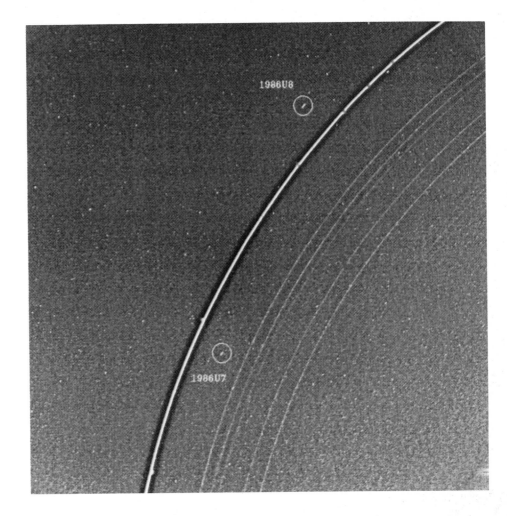

Although Voyager found Uranus almost featureless, the visit was not in vain. Besides discovering ten new Uranian moons and obtaining close-up photographs of the five known ones, Voyager was able to distinguish ten very narrow rings of particles in Uranus's ring system. The rings are widely separated by several shepherd satellites that were among the ten new moons found by Voyager.

Particles in the rings are made of ice but are covered with sootlike material, which makes them appear very dark. Most of the particles are about the size of a fist or bigger. One would expect to find smaller particles as well, possibly as small as dust. Astronomers theorize that some process must be sweeping the rings clear, leaving only the larger chunks.

Uranus now has fifteen known moons. Its most bizarre is Miranda, which was discovered forty years ago. None of Uranus's five major satellites is very big, but Miranda is the smallest.

Voyager discovered that Miranda's surface has a bewildering display of land forms, including vast cracks exposing giant cliffs. One cliff is nearly 20 kilometers (12 miles) high. The Grand Canyon in Arizona is a little more than 1/2 kilometer (1 mile) deep. Since Miranda is only 480 kilometers (300 miles) in diameter, its cliff must truly loom above the landscape.

Another feature on Miranda looks like a large bright check mark or number 7. It is sometimes called the chevron. There are also two huge oval features near Miranda's equator. These have been nicknamed *circi maximi* because they resemble the ancient Roman chariot-racing tracks.

One possible explanation for Miranda's strange appearance is that, while it was still young, it was broken up into many pieces of rock and ice. These chunks stayed close together in orbit and eventually collected again into a single body, but the reorganization was very haphazard, making Miranda look like a crazy jigsaw puzzle today.

The astronomers would have liked Voyager to linger longer at Uranus. But even as the spacecraft approached Uranus, they were preparing speed and direction commands to be radioed to it. With a gravity-assist from Uranus, Voyager would head toward Neptune.

(Above) Miranda's rugged surface as seen from 35,000 kilometers (22,000 miles) away. Note the high cliff on the lower right horizon and the 24-kilometer (15-mile)-wide crater at the lower left. Above the crater is grooved terrain. (Right) A mosaic (composite) photograph of Uranus's strange moon Miranda from an average distance of 35,000 kilometers (22,000 miles) away, showing its varied geologic regions. (Below) Miranda's chevron figure at lower left contrasts with the curved grooves in the opposite corner.

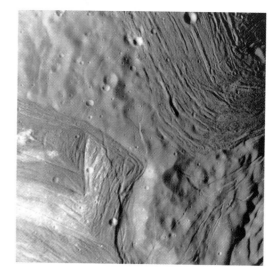

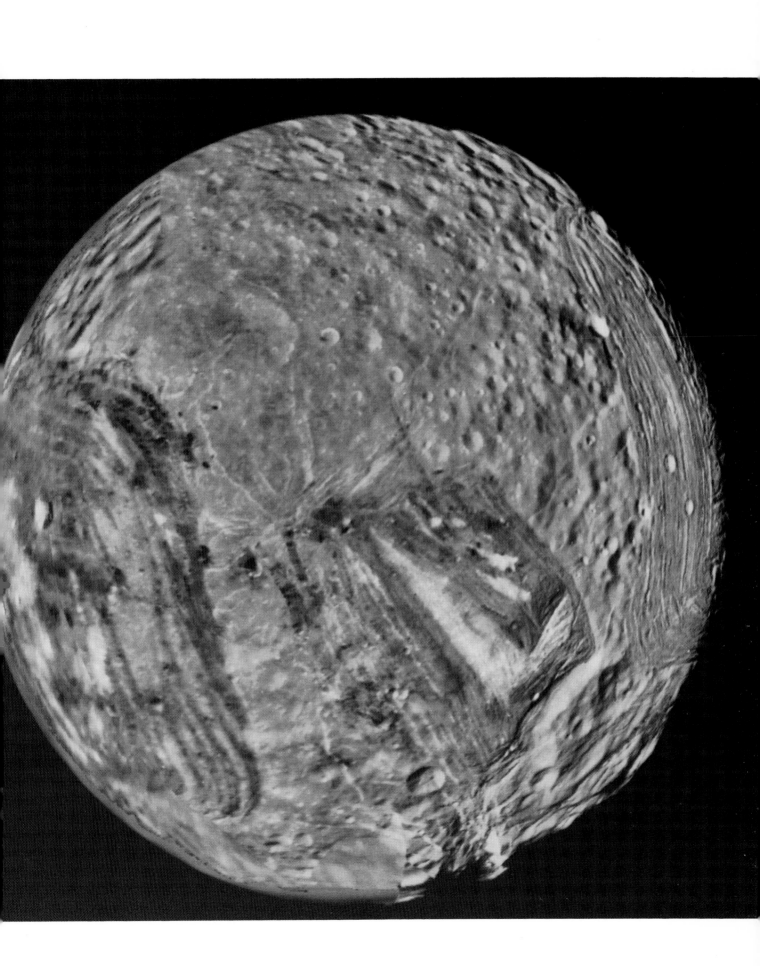

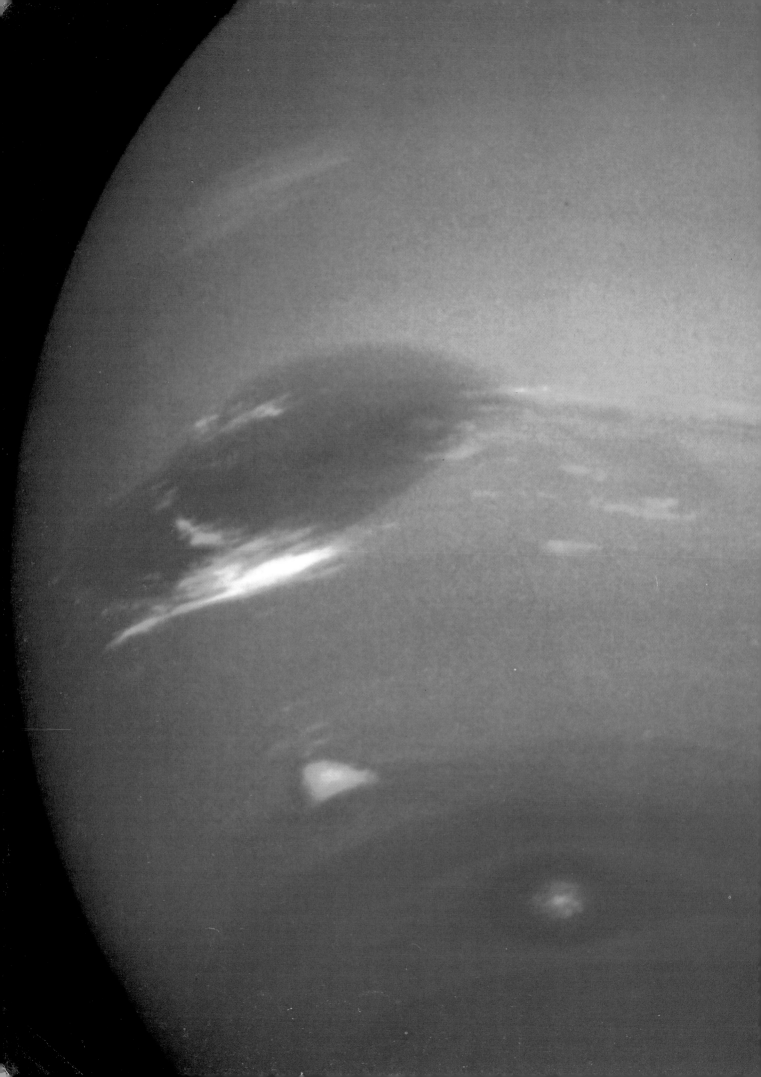

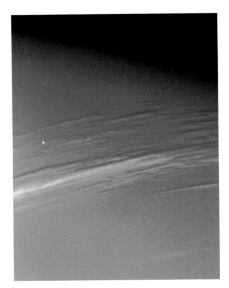

(Above) High-altitude cloud streaks in Neptune's atmosphere. Note the shadows they cast. (Left) A view of the planet Neptune showing its three major storm areas within its turbulent clouds. The Great Dark Spot lies near the equator with the triangular storm called Scooter just below it. Dark Spot Two is at lower right.

By the time Voyager arrived at Neptune, the engineers were already jokingly describing the spacecraft as being hard of hearing with a touch of arthritis and a slight loss of memory. Voyager was a very old spacecraft indeed.

However, Voyager came closer to Neptune than it did to any other object in its long journey. It passed 4,400 kilometers (2,700 miles) above the cloud tops over Neptune's north pole. That was on August 25, 1989, twelve years after its launch. Voyager was now 4½ billion kilometers (2¾ billion miles) from Earth. The spacecraft was so far from the people who sent commands to it that it would have to operate at the very limit of its capability to hear their directions.

Neptune is too far away from us to be seen without a telescope. Sunlight reaching Uranus is very dim, but it is two and a half times as much as the amount of light reaching Neptune. Neptune receives only one-thousandth the amount of light we receive on Earth.

Astronomers thought that Neptune would be featureless like Uranus. They were delightfully surprised. Neptune is about the same size as Uranus and shares the same blue-green color because of a small amount of methane in its clouds. But heat rising from Neptune's hot interior keeps its cloud top temperatures similar to Uranus's temperatures, even though Neptune is more than a billion miles farther away from the sun.

This rising heat drives fierce winds, creating huge storms in Neptune's atmosphere, much like those found on Jupiter. Instead of finding a peaceful-looking planet, Voyager found active cloud structures in a turbulent state.

A close-up of Neptune's Great Dark Spot, a giant storm system

Neptune's biggest feature is called the Great Dark Spot, which is a huge rotating storm about the size of Earth. Unlike Jupiter's Great Red Spot, the Great Dark Spot is a hole or depression in the clouds. It lets us look deep into Neptune's atmosphere, although all we see is darker shades of Neptune's blue-green methane covering.

About 50 kilometers (30 miles) above the atmosphere, white cirruslike clouds form and dissipate around the Great Dark Spot, similar to the way clouds form on mountainsides on Earth. White wispy clouds are also found near a small triangular-shaped storm, which moves around the planet faster than the Great Dark Spot and has therefore been dubbed Scooter. Another storm, Dark Spot Two, is smaller than the Great Dark Spot and is oval in shape. It has a white cloud hovering above its center.

The thick blue-green clouds covering Uranus and Neptune make up only about 10 to 20 percent of the planets' mass. The rest is rock and ice beneath the clouds. Uranus and Neptune are not true gas planets like Jupiter and Saturn. Scientists believe that they may be the accumulation of thousands of huge boulders that crashed together and formed planets early in the solar system's history.

After Voyager confirmed that both Jupiter and Uranus had ring systems, astronomers were fairly sure that Neptune would have one, too. They were, therefore, not surprised when Voyager detected it. When the spacecraft was still far away from Neptune, the pictures it sent back to Earth showed only sections of rings. Not until Voyager was much closer could the rest of the rings be observed. The brighter sections seen at first were found simply to have more material in them, making them more visible. And once again, Voyager detected shepherd satellites confining two of the first three rings it discovered into very narrow areas. The third ring is much more spread out. Later, after studying Voyager's photographs more closely, astronomers discovered a fourth and fifth ring.

Neptune's ring system, shown in two exposures lasting nearly ten minutes each

Voyager also found six new moons orbiting Neptune, raising the total number known to eight. But most amazing was what Voyager discovered about Triton, Neptune's largest moon. Although Triton had been observed from Earth many years before, little was known about it other than that it was one of the largest satellites in the solar system. Triton orbits Neptune in a retrograde motion, which means that it goes around Neptune in the direction opposite to Neptune's spin. It is the only major moon in the solar system to have this characteristic, although some of the smaller moons of Jupiter have retrograde motion.

The surface of Triton, as revealed by Voyager, is fascinating. Bright snowfalls only a few decades old contrast with craters billions of years old. In general, however, craters are very scarce on Triton, indicating that its crust is quite young and is constantly changing.

Voyager found several active volcanoes on Triton. The material coming from them is not molten rock like the hot lava that comes out of volcanoes on Earth. Instead, water mixed with other substances is spewed out, making the volcanoes more like geysers.

Voyager also photographed dark plumes of dust-filled nitrogen gas erupting from beneath Triton's surface. The gas rises some 8 kilometers (5 miles) into the thin atmosphere before being blown more than 240 kilometers (150 miles) across the moon. The dark plumes are seen as streaks of black on the much lighter landscape.

(Above) View of about 480 kilometers (300 miles) of the surface of Neptune's largest moon, Triton. (Right) Mosaic (composite) photograph of Triton. (Below) Triton's south pole area. About fifty dark plumes mark what may be ice volcanoes.

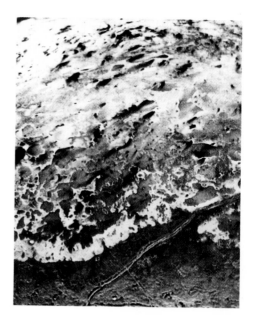

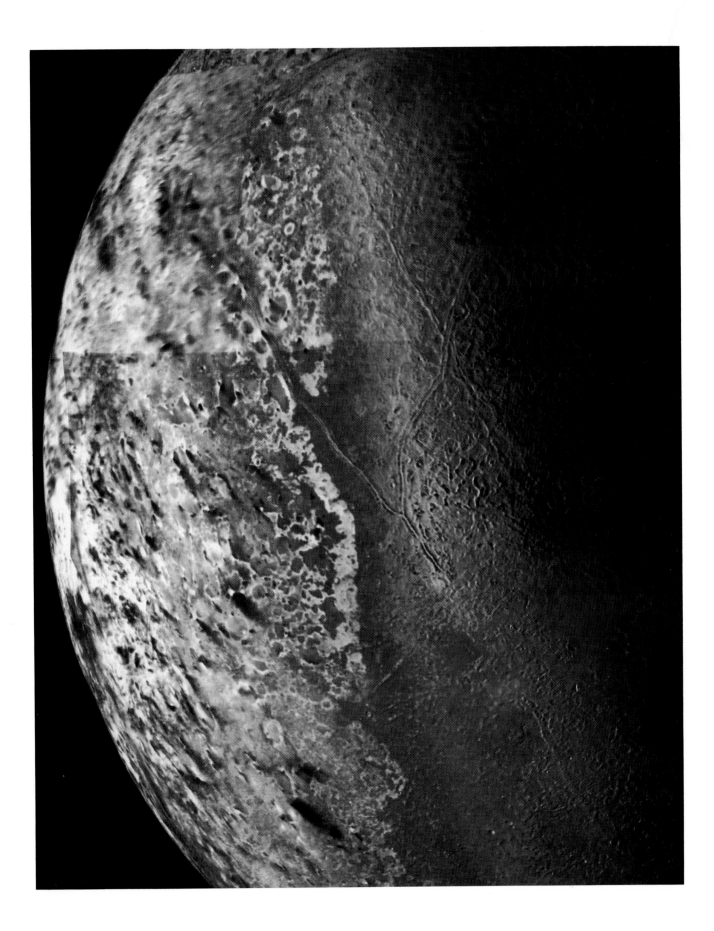

Triton's southern polar cap was almost perfectly white, covered with frozen nitrogen, when Voyager passed by. A photograph of the region closer to Triton's equator showed where this ice was starting to melt and where, farther north, nitrogen frost was starting to form. Seasonal changes on Triton are very long and slow, but they do keep altering this moon's features. The central or equatorial zone on Triton is darker than the rest of the surface and has a dimpled texture much like that of a cantaloupe rind. There Voyager found long thin ridges where the crust had broken and thick slush had oozed out and frozen.

After Voyager 2 passed Neptune, its program was given a new name—Voyager Interstellar Mission (VIM)—because now it is headed out of the solar system, out to the stars. It should continue transmitting data until at least the year 2010, when it will be at the outer boundary of the sun's energy influence. This is a region where the stream of particles constantly being emitted by the sun is stopped by collisions with particles in interstellar space. This boundary is called the heliopause.

Very little will change on Voyager as it sails on through outer space. Eventually its electrical power will be used up and its instruments will cease to function, but there is nothing in space that will stop Voyager from traveling farther and farther from us. Only when it comes close enough to be affected by another star's gravitational attraction will its path be altered. Astronomers have calculated that that won't happen for at least twenty-seven thousand years!

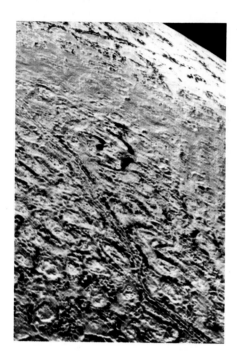

(Above) Triton from 40,000 kilometers (25,000 miles) away. Depressions may be caused by melting and collapsing of the icy surface. The long feature is probably a narrow fault line. (Right) Voyager took this photograph three days after its flyby of Neptune and Triton.

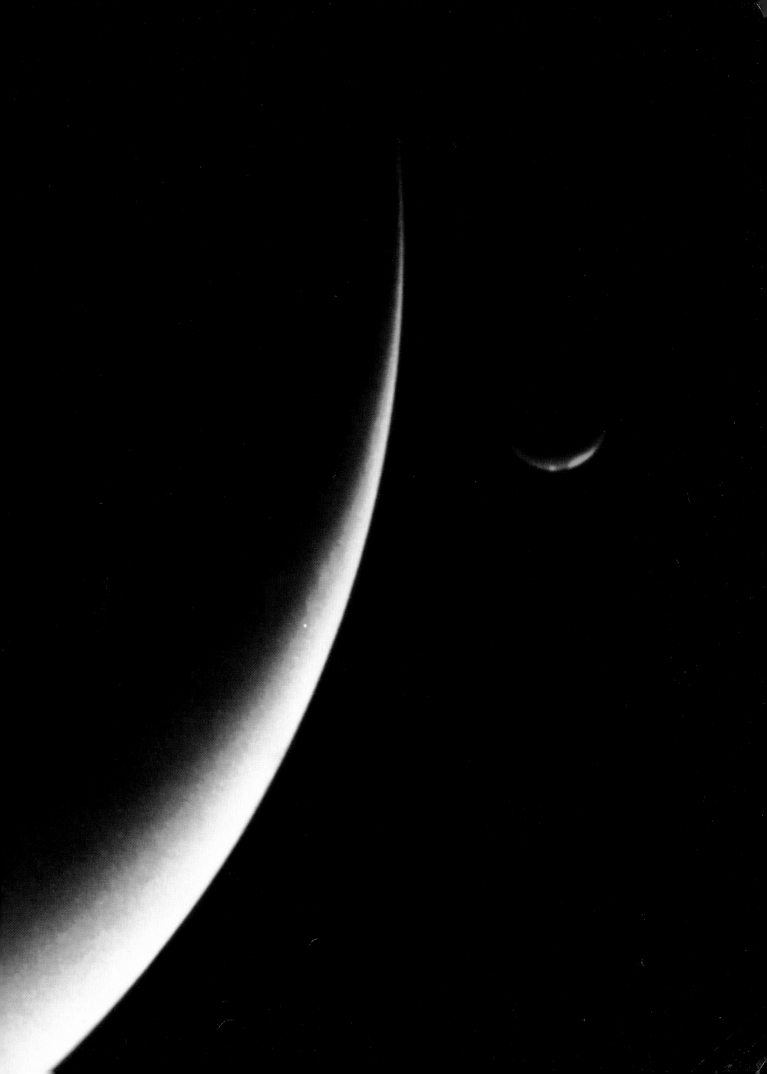

(Left) A crowded star field in our galaxy, the Milky Way. (Right) The gold phonograph record attached to the side of the Voyager spacecraft. It can be seen in its special cover in the photograph of the spacecraft on page 10.

We don't know if there are any intelligent beings elsewhere in the universe, but if there are—and if they find either of the two Voyagers wandering out in space—they will discover, in addition to all the instruments, a very special gold-plated record on the side of each spacecraft. On each record is a recorded greeting from the people on Earth in fifty-five languages as well as many sounds that are common on Earth. These include the roar of a jet plane, the crying of babies, the chirping of crickets, and ninety minutes of a variety of music. Covering this precious record is a diagram showing what Earth people look like and where Earth is in the solar system. The story of Voyager will be an ancient legend before any alien being can possibly find the spacecraft. But maybe, many thousands of years from now...

INDEX

Callisto, 7, 19
Cape Canaveral, 8
Chevron, Miranda, 36
Circi maximi, 36
Craters, 18, 19, 28

Dark Spot Two, 40
Deep Space Network, 31

Enceladus, 29
Europa, 7, 16–17

Galilean moons, 15–19
Galileo, 15, 21
Ganymede, 7, 18
Grand Tour, 7–8
Gravity-assists, 7, 8, 30, 36
Great Dark Spot, 39, 40
Great Red Spot, 14–15

Heliopause, 44
Herschel, Sir William, 32
Hyperion, 29

Io, 16

Jupiter, 7, 8
  clouds, 12–14
  Great Red Spot, 14–15
  moons, 15–19
  rings, 20–21

Mariner 2, 7
Mimas, 28
Miranda, 33, 36
Moons
  of Jupiter, 15–19, 21
  of Neptune, 42–44
  of Saturn, 26–29
  of Uranus, 32, 35, 36

NASA, 8
Neptune, 8, 30, 39–41
  moons, 42–44
  rings, 21, 41
  storm clouds, 40

Radio telescopes, 31
Record, on spacecraft, 47
Rings
  of Jupiter, 20–21
  of Neptune, 21, 41
  of Saturn, 21, 23–25
  of Uranus, 21, 32, 35

Saturn, 8, 22
  moons, 26–29
  rings, 21, 23–25
Scooter, 39, 40
Shepherd satellites, 21, 25, 26, 35, 41

Tethys, 28–29
Titan, 8, 26–27
Triton, 42–44

Uranus, 8, 21, 30–35
  moons, 32, 35, 36
  rings, 21

Venus, 7
Very Large Array (VLA), 31
Volcanoes, 16, 42–44
Voyager, 8, 11–12, 30–32
Voyager Interstellar Mission (VIM), 44

FURTHER READING

Ardley, Neil. *The Outer Planets.* New York: Schoolhouse Press, Inc. (Dist.: Simon & Schuster), 1988.

Asimov, Isaac. *Jupiter: The Spotted Giant.* Milwaukee: Gareth Stevens Inc., 1989.

_____. *Neptune: The Farthest Giant.* Milwaukee: Gareth Stevens Inc., 1990.

_____. *Uranus: The Sideways Planet.* Milwaukee: Gareth Stevens Inc., 1988.

Branley, Franklyn M. *Saturn: The Spectacular Planet.* Illustrated by Leonard Kessler. New York: Harper Junior Books, 1987.

_____. *Uranus: The Seventh Planet.* Illustrated by Yvonne Buchanan. New York: Harper Junior Books, 1988.

Odyssey magazine, published monthly by Kalmbach Publishing Co., P.O. Box 1612, Waukesha, Wisconsin 53187.

PRONUNCIATION GUIDE

Callisto   kuh LISS toe

Enceladus   en sell AH dus

Europa   you ROPE a

Ganymede   GAN ih meed

Hyperion   hi PIRR ee on

Io   EYE o

Mimas   MY mus

Tethys   TEETH iss

Titan   TIE tun

Triton   TRY tun

Uranus   YOO rah nuss